100
of the Coolest Words in the World

by

Sydney Spence

Hello I am Sydney Spence. I love words and I love cool things which is what brought me to create a unique collection of books that are insightful and thought-provoking. This is the first book of my 100 Cool Things series. From participating in spelling bees to researching and learning new words, I have always been a logophile. Hope you enjoy!

Aspectabund

(adjective) Latin

letting or being able to let expressive emotion
show easily through ones face and eyes

Aesthete
(noun) Greek

someone with deep sensitivity to the beauty of
art or nature

Atermoiements
(noun) French

distractions of hesitations leading to
procrastination

Alexithymia
(noun) Greek

the inability to express your feelings

Abience
(noun) Latin

the strong urge to avoid someone or something

Balter

(verb)

to dance artlessly without particular grace or
skill but usually with enjoyment

Bibliophilia
(noun) French

the love of books

Bedgasm
(noun)

a feeling of euphoria experienced when
climbing into bed at the end of a very long day

Boketto

(verb) Japanese

the act of gazing vacantly into the distance
without a thought

Burgeon
(verb) French

begin to grow or increase rapidly; flourish

Concinnity

(noun) Latin

harmony or elegance of design

Cosmogryal
(adjective) English

whirling around the universe

Cicatrize
(verb) Old French

to find healing by the process of forming scars

Chrysalism
(noun)

the amniotic tranquility of being indoors
during a thunderstorm

Drapetomania
(noun) Greek

an overwhelming urge to run away

Depaysement
(noun) French

when someone is taken out of their own
familiar world into a new one

Dormiveglia
(noun)

the space that stretches between sleeping and
waking

Destinesia
(noun)

when you get to where you were intending to
go, but forgot why you were going there in the
first place

Eccedentesiast
(noun) Latin

someone who hides pain behind a smile

Elysian
(adjective)

beautiful or creative; divinely inspired;
peaceful and perfect

Eremophobia
(noun) Greek

the deep fear of stillness

Eleutheromania
(adjective)

an intense and irresistible desire for freedom

Engentado
(adjective)

feeling "peopled out" and wishing to be alone

Epiphany
(noun) Old French

a moment of sudden revelation

Fantods
(noun)

state of extreme anxiety, distress

Finifugal
(adjective)

hating endings; someone who tries to avoid or prolong the final moments of a story, relationship, or some other journey

Gibel

Russian

ceasing to exist; deteriorating in a way that is
painful for others

Gerascophobia
(noun)

the fear of growing old

Gallimaufry
(noun) French

a confused jumble

Gigil
(noun)

the irresistible urge to squeeze someone
because you love them

Hippopotomonstrosesquippedaliophobia
(noun)

the fear of long words

Halcyon
(adjective) Latin

calm and peaceful; happy prosperous

Hiraeth

(noun) Welsh

a homesickness for a home you can't return to,
or that never was

Hygge
(noun) Danish

a deep sense of place, warmth, friendship, and
contentment

Heliophilia
(noun)

desire to stay in the sun; love of sunlight

Induratize
(verb)

to make one's own heart hardened or resistant
to someone's pleas or advances, or the idea of
love

Irenic

(adjective) Greek

promoting peace

Icarus
(noun) Greek

thee who flew too close to the sun

Ilunga
(noun)

a person who is willing to forgive someone's mistake the first time' tolerate it the second time, but never a third time

Ineffable
(adjective)

too great to be expressed in words

Ikigai
Japanese

a reason for being; the thing that gets you up
in the morning

Jaaneman
(noun)

gender neutral word for sweetheart or darling

Jayus
(noun) Indonesian

a joke so unfunny and poorly old that you can't
help but laugh

Jouska
(noun)

a hypothetical conversation that you
compulsively play out in your head

Kalon

(noun)

beauty that is more than skin-deep

Komorebi

Japanese

sunlight that filters through the leaves of trees

Kadota
(verb)

to disappear; vanish

Lacuna

(noun) Latin

a blank space

Laconic

(adjective) Latin

expressing much in few words

Ludic

(adjective) French

full of fun and high spirits

Logophile

(noun) Greek

a lover of words

Lethologica
(noun) Greek

when you can't think of the word for
something

Laotong

(noun) Chinese

a friendship bonding 2 girls together for
eternity as kindred sisters

Logastellus

(noun) Greek

a person whose love of words is greater

Metanoia
(noun) Greek

the journey of changing ones mind, heart, self,
or way of life

Meraki
(verb)

to do something with soul creativity, or love

Magoa
(noun) Portuguse

a heart breaking feeling that leaves long-lasting
traces, visible in gestures, and facial expression

Mudita

(noun) Sanskrit

taking delight in the happiness of others

Majime

(noun) Japanese

an earnest, reliable person who can simply get
things done without causing drama

Nazlanmak
(verb) Turkish

pretending reluctance or indifference when
you are actually willing or eager; saying no and
meaning yes

Nubivagant
(adjective) Latin

moving among clouds

Nyctophilia
(noun)

love of darkness or night; finding relaxation or
comfort in the darkness

Nemesism
(noun)

frustration, anger, or aggression directed
inward toward oneself and ones way of living

Novaturient

(adjective) Latin

a desire to alter your life; the feeling that
pushes you to travel

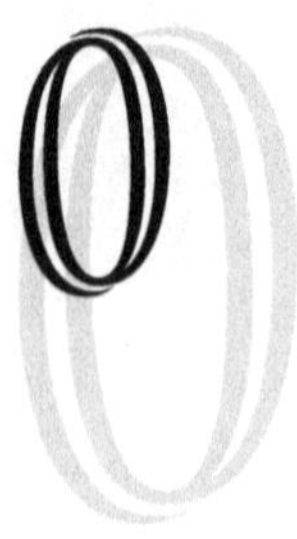

Onism

(noun)

the awareness of how little of the world you'll experience

Ostranenie

(noun) Russian

encouraging people to see common things as strange, wild, or unfamiliar

Oneirataxia

(noun) Greek

the inability to distinguish between fantasy
and reality;

mysterious and entrancing; beyond ordinary
understanding

Palinoia

(noun) Greek

the obsessive repetition of an act until it is
perfect or mastered

Petrichor
(noun) Greek

the smell of earth after rain

Psithurism

(noun) Antient Greek

the sound of wind in the trees and rustling of
leaves

Paracosm

(noun) Antient Greek

a detailed prolonged imaginary world created
by a child that includes human, animal, or
alien creations

Quatervois

(noun)

a critical decision or turning point in one's life

Quiddity
(noun) Latin

the essence of something

Quierencia
(noun) Spanish

a place from which one's strength is drawn,
where one feels at home

Quaintrelle
(noun) French

a woman who emphasized a life of passion, expressed through personal style, leisurely pastimes, charm, and cultivation of lifes pleasures

Rantipole
(adjective)

wild and reckless

Resol

(noun) Spanish

the reflection of sunlight off a surface

Solivagant
(adjective) Latin

wandering and alone

Serendipity
(noun)

finding something good without looking for it

Sarang
(verb)

the feeling of wanting to be with someone
until death

Tacenda

(noun) Latin

things better left unsaid; matters to be passed
over in silence

Thalassophile
(noun) Greek

a lover of the sea, someone who loves the sea,
ocean

Trouvaille

(noun) French

something lovely discovered by chance

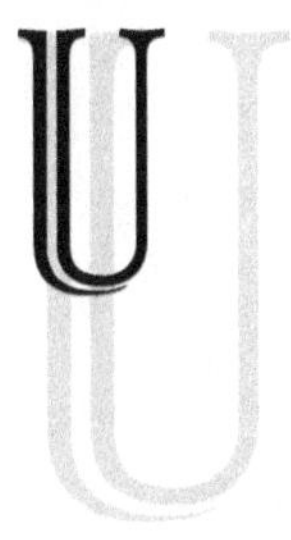

Ubiquitous

(adjective) Latin

present, appearing or found everywhere

Ukiyo

(noun) Japanese

living in the moment, detached from the
bothers of life

Vad

(noun)

wild, untamed

Velleitie

(noun) Latin

a wish or powerful desire for something that
nonetheless is not or cannot be followed by
actions meant to pursue it

Verendus
(adjective) Latin

to be feared, worthy of reverence, giving an
impression of aged goodness and benevolence

Wabi-sabi

(noun) Japanese

the discovery of beauty in imperfection; the
acceptance of the cycle of life and death

Wanderlust

(noun) German

a strong desire to travel and explore the world

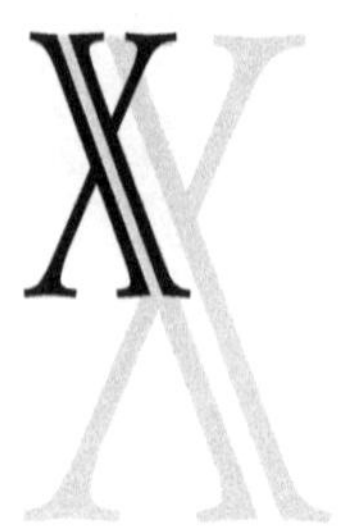

Xenophile
(noun)

one attracted to foreign things

Xenization

(noun)

the act of existing as a stranger

Xenodocheionology

love of hotels and inns

Yatta

(interjection) Japanese

the state of joy after you accomplish a task

Yoisho

(noun) Japanese

a word without meaning

Yeoubi

(noun) Korean

the sun shining through rain

Z

Zeal
(noun)

energy and enthusiasm for something

Zest
(noun)

an exciting quality or keen enjoyment

Zugzwang
(noun) German

a situation where every possible move or
decision is a bad one, or one that will result in
damage or loss